I LOVE CARS

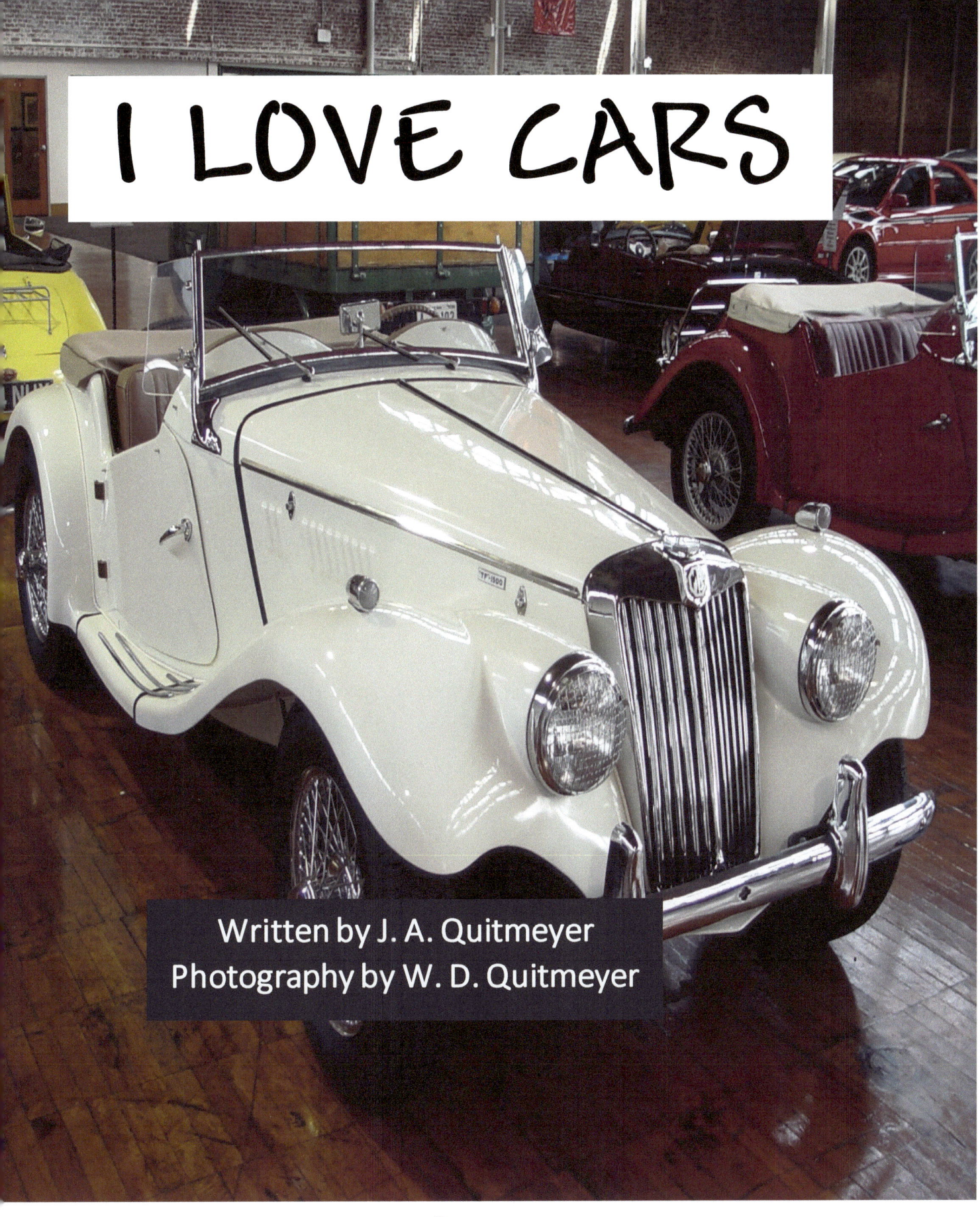

Written by J. A. Quitmeyer
Photography by W. D. Quitmeyer

Text Copyright ©2021 by JoAnn A. Quitmeyer
Photography Copyright ©2021 by Wallace D. Quitmeyer

All cars photographed here were on display at the Lane Motor Museum located on Murfreesboro Pike in Nashville, Tennessee.

Printed in the United States of America.
10 9 8 7 6 5 4 3 2 1

ISBN 978-1-945450-14-3

All rights reserved. No part of this book may be used or reproduced in any manner whatsoever without written permission except in brief quotations embodied in critical articles and reviews.

For information contact Baird Farms Publishing Co.
Mount Juliet, TN. 37122
wdjaq@aol.com

This book is dedicated to the memory of Wally Quitmeyer, my husband of 50 years, and an avid photographer. It also is dedicated to Mr. Jeff Lane and The Lane Car Museum who so lovingly collected this broad spectrum of cars that otherwise we would never have seen.

J.

Places near,
Places far,
Go anywhere
In this little car.

Some cars are old,
Some cars are new,
Some cars are yellow
And some are blue.

This little green car
Has a great big grill;
Hop in for a ride
That is sure to thrill.

This little red car
Opens to the sky,
Go up the mountain;
Climb very high.

Step up close;
Let's go for a ride.
Hop right in and
Sit by my side.

We will go
So many places,
With broad smiles
Upon our faces.

A racy roadster
Is just the thing;
A short little ride
Will make us sing.

Topless, small and
Shiny white,
Wind in our hair
And all is right.

This is a big world
For us to see;
Best friends forever,
Just you and me.

This shiny blue
Limousine
Is one of the finest
That I've ever seen.

Lots of room
In the front and back,
You can seat the whole family,
Even the cat.

Snow shoes, ski boots,
Fishing tackle and poles,
You can pack all you need,
Whatever your goals.

This fancy ragtop
Automobile
Makes visions soar
And wishes real.

Step inside;
Get ready to ride;
No need to hide;
Just smile wide.

We are feeling great,
Don't want to be late,
Adventurous fate,
I can hardly wait!

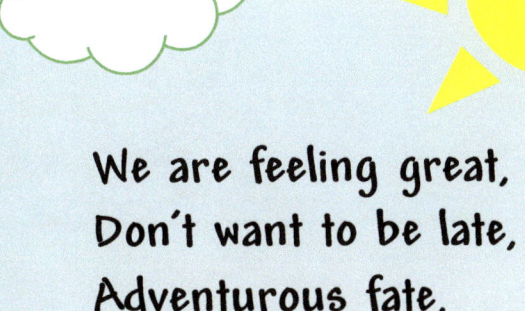

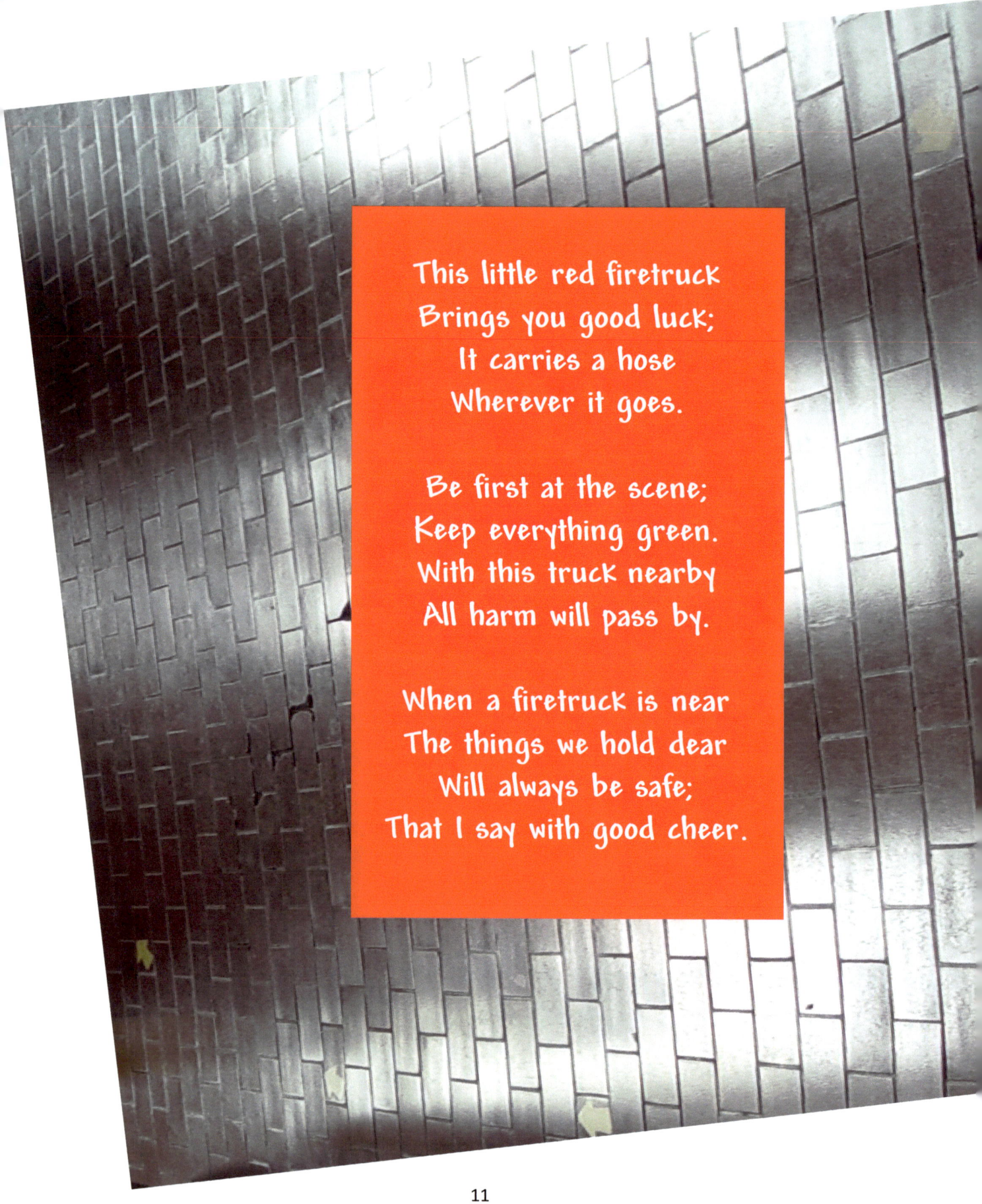

This little red firetruck
Brings you good luck;
It carries a hose
Wherever it goes.

Be first at the scene;
Keep everything green.
With this truck nearby
All harm will pass by.

When a firetruck is near
The things we hold dear
Will always be safe;
That I say with good cheer.

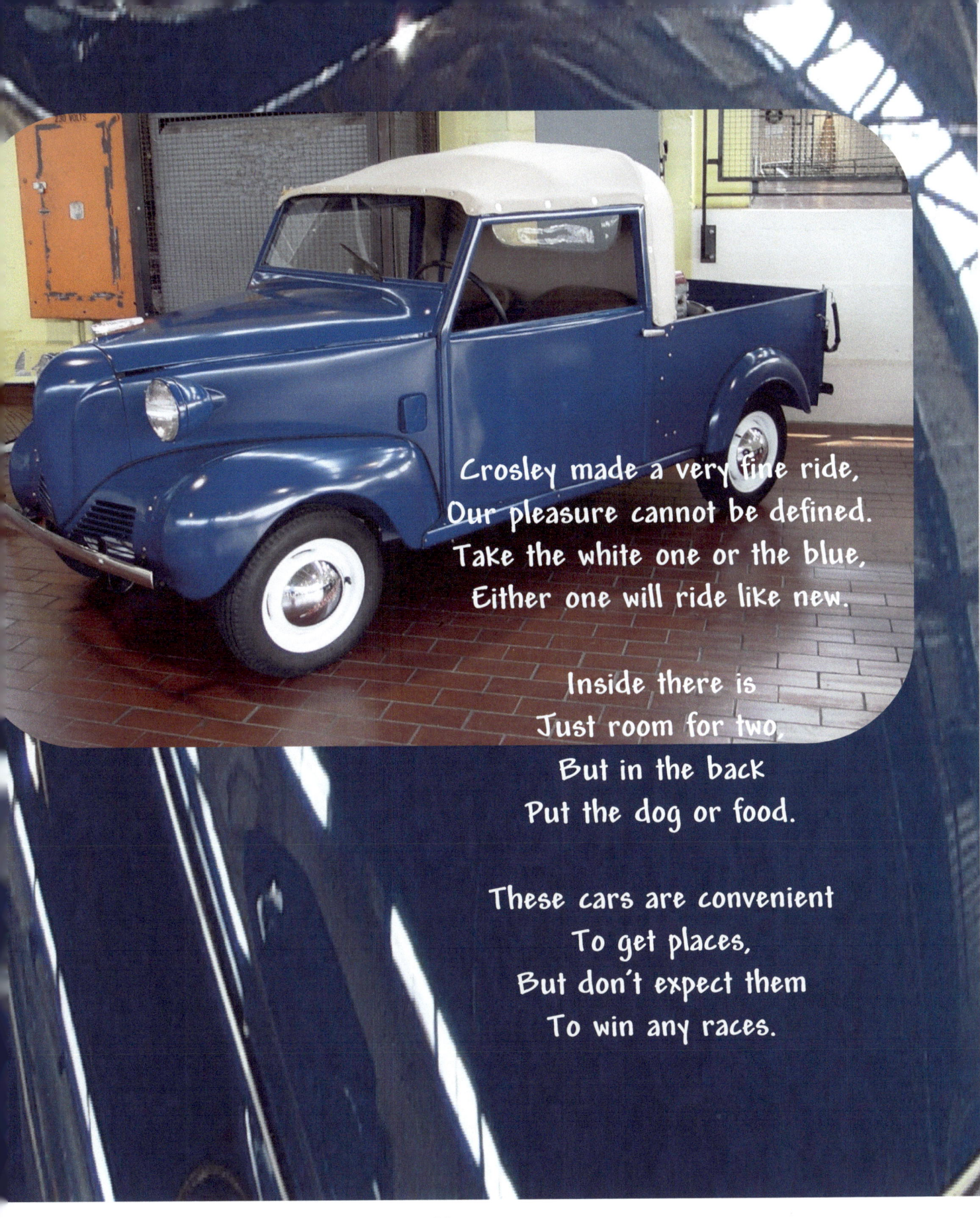

Crosley made a very fine ride,
Our pleasure cannot be defined.
Take the white one or the blue,
Either one will ride like new.

Inside there is
Just room for two,
But in the back
Put the dog or food.

These cars are convenient
To get places,
But don't expect them
To win any races.

This yellow car with
Big red wheels,
Is a perfect ride
To get our thrills.

A classy roadster,
It's built just for two.
If we sit very close
It will hold me and you.

Climb aboard
Without any cares,
We will go very fast,
The wind in our hair.

Some cars go fast,
Some cars go slow,
Some cars are built
To glide on snow.

In the back
Is a giant fan,
It spins so fast
Like a wound
Rubber band.

Take a good look
Before we go.
This may be the last time
To see such a show.

This three-wheeled car,
With a picnic basket,
Will take us far but
You may need a jacket.

Hop in by my side
And snuggle close;
The top is down and I
Have frost on my nose.

This tiny three-wheeled
Automobile
Is so cute,
It doesn't look real.

Go for a ride
With a friend or two;
It's a real sure way
To shake the blues.

The End!

JoAnn Quitmeyer has authored numerous articles published in technical journals, authored technical chapters and most recently authored "Modern Industrial Cleaning," published by Same Old Story Publishing and soon to be re-released by Baird Farms Publishing Company LLC.

She recently authored the book, "I Love Trains," published by Baird Farms Publishing Co. LLC.

Under the pseudonym E. Emma Zimmer, JoAnn Quitmeyer has also authored a number of children's books including "Annabelle Anteater's First Day of School" published by Same Old Story Publishing. She also illustrated "PURPLE," authored by Joseph R. Hornsby. Both are soon to be re-released by Baird Farms Publishing under J. A. Quitmeyer.

www.ingramcontent.com/pod-product-compliance
Lightning Source LLC
Chambersburg PA
CBHW041504220426
43661CB00016B/1245